Jenny was sad.

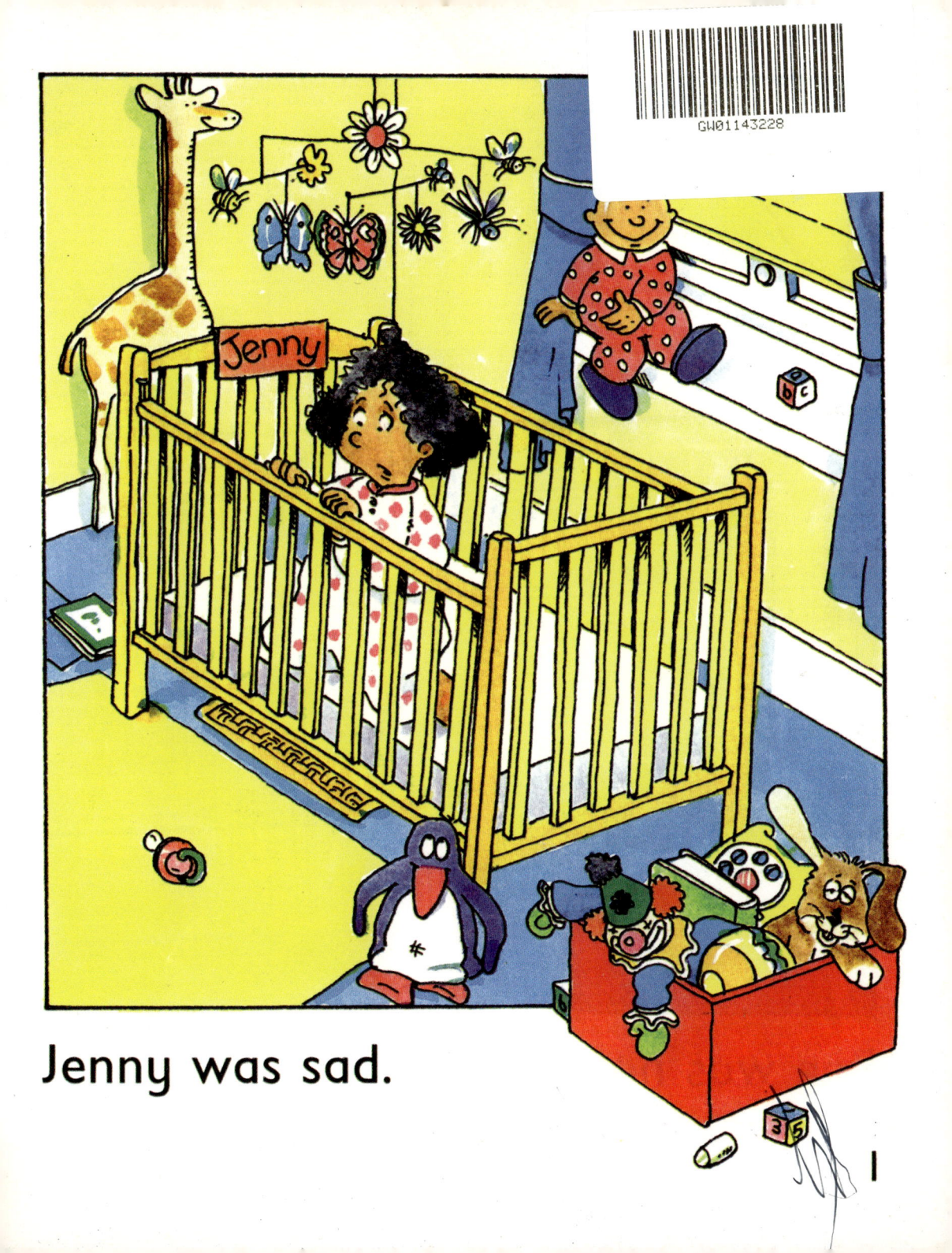

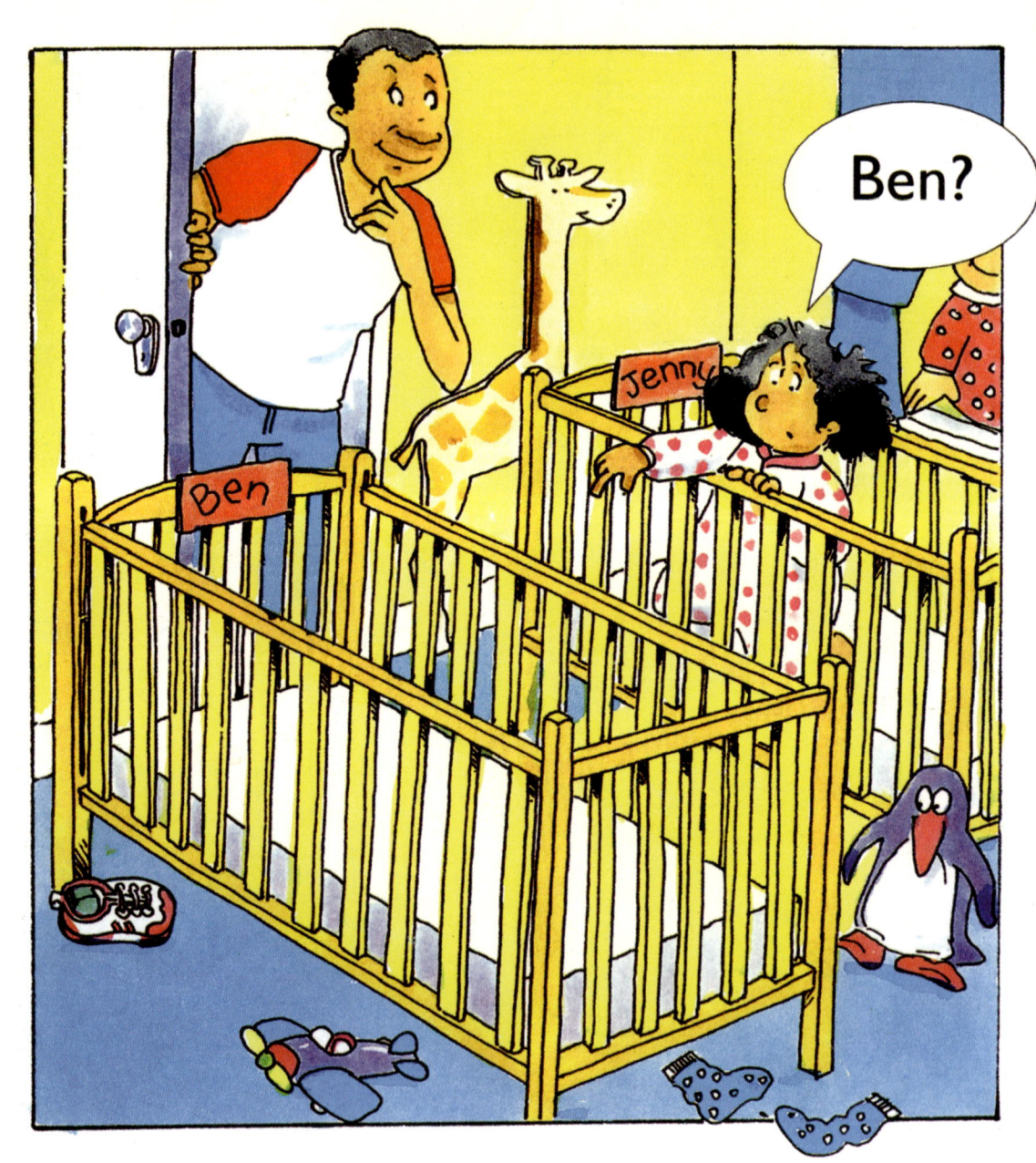

Ben was not in his cot.

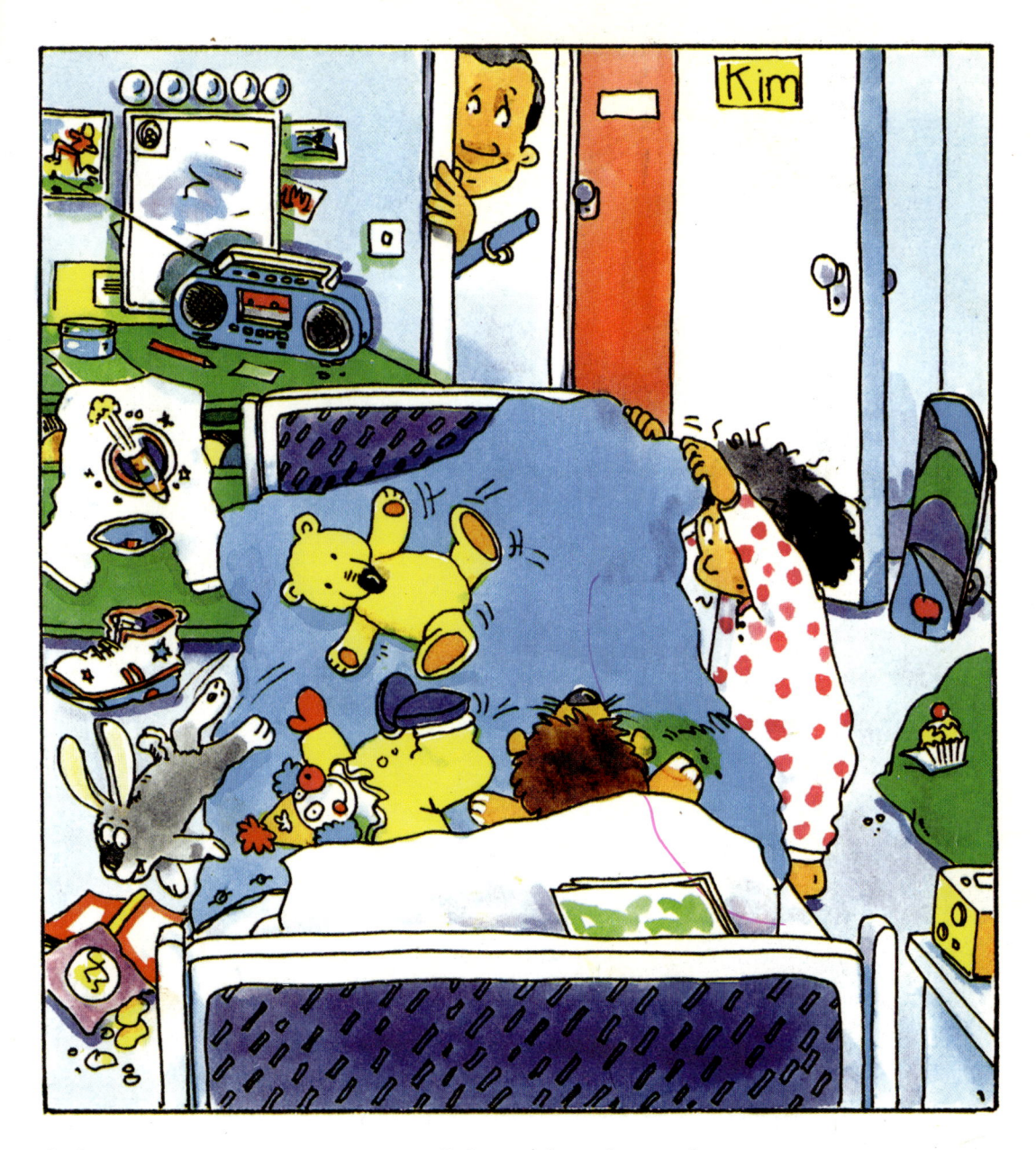

He was not in Kim's bed.

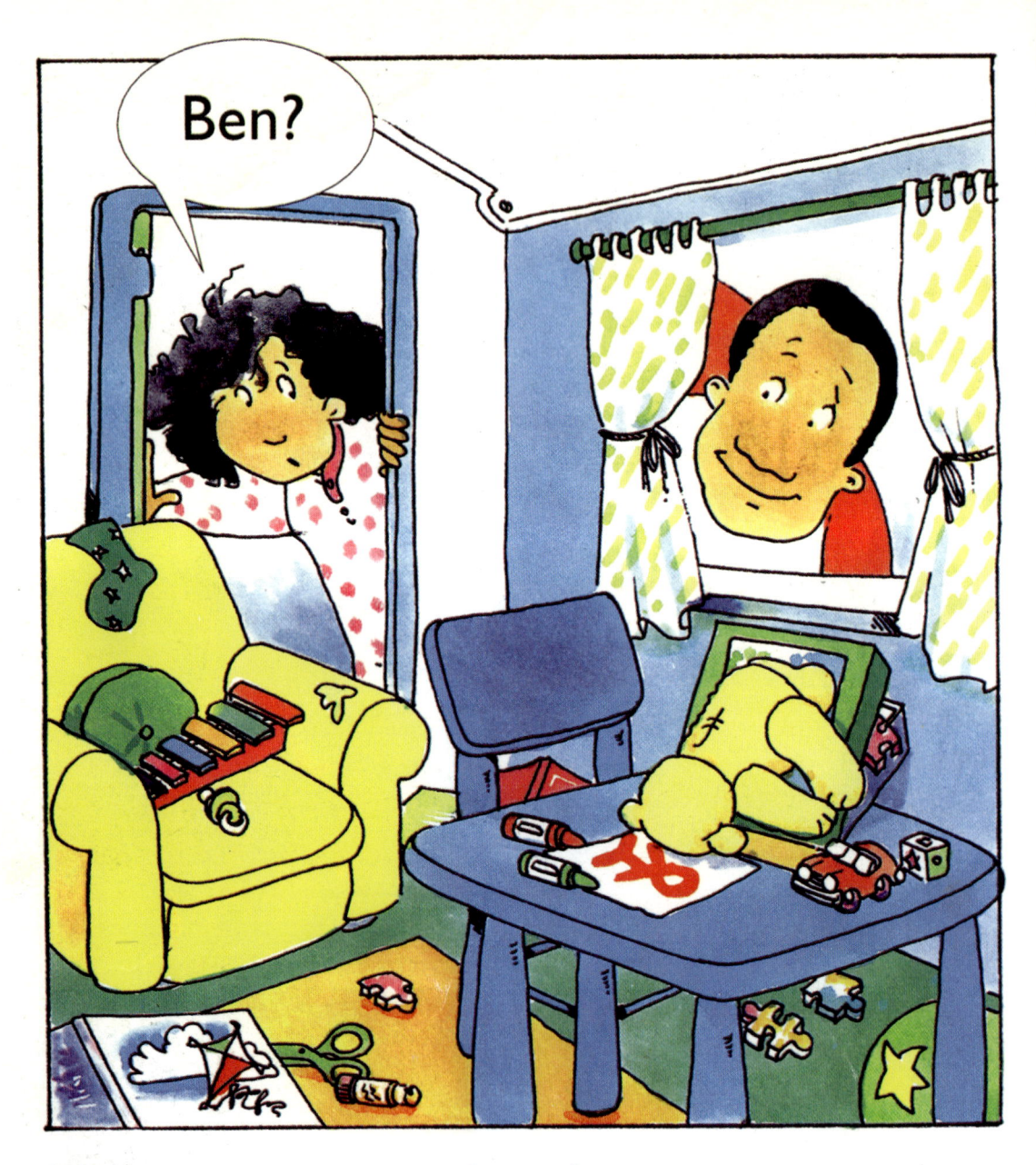

He was not in the den.

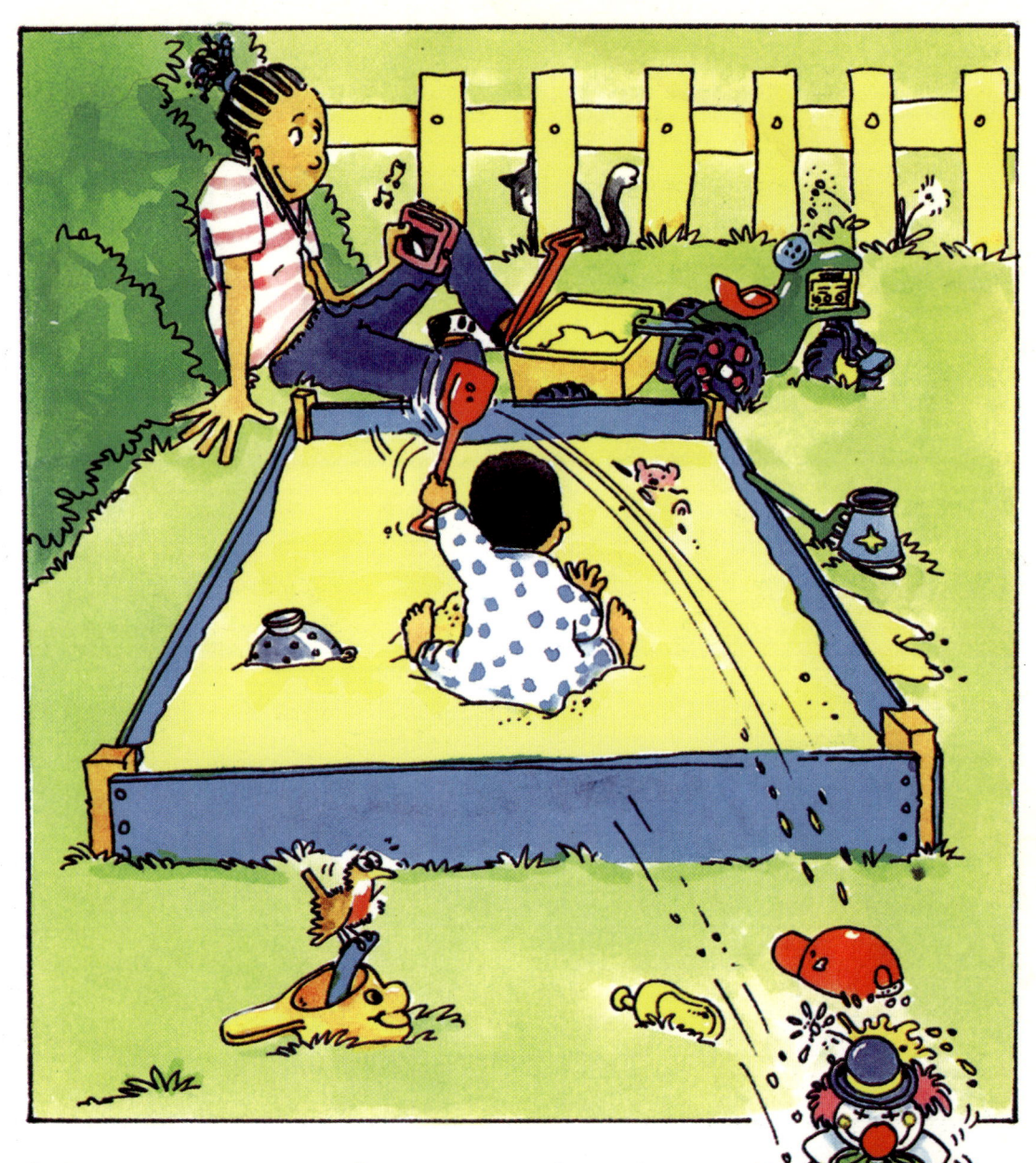

He was in the sandpit.

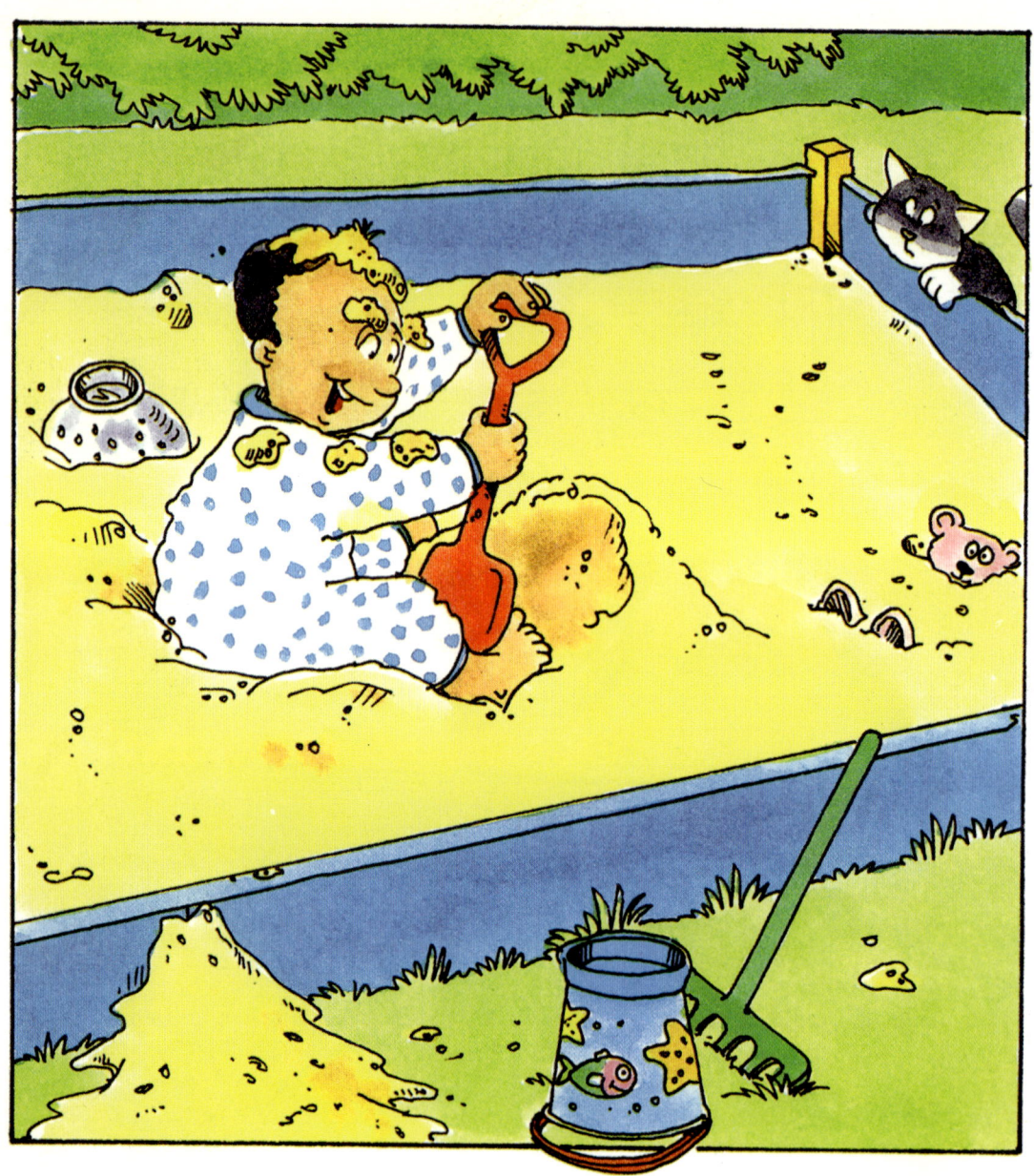

Ben had sand on him.

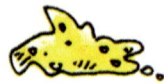

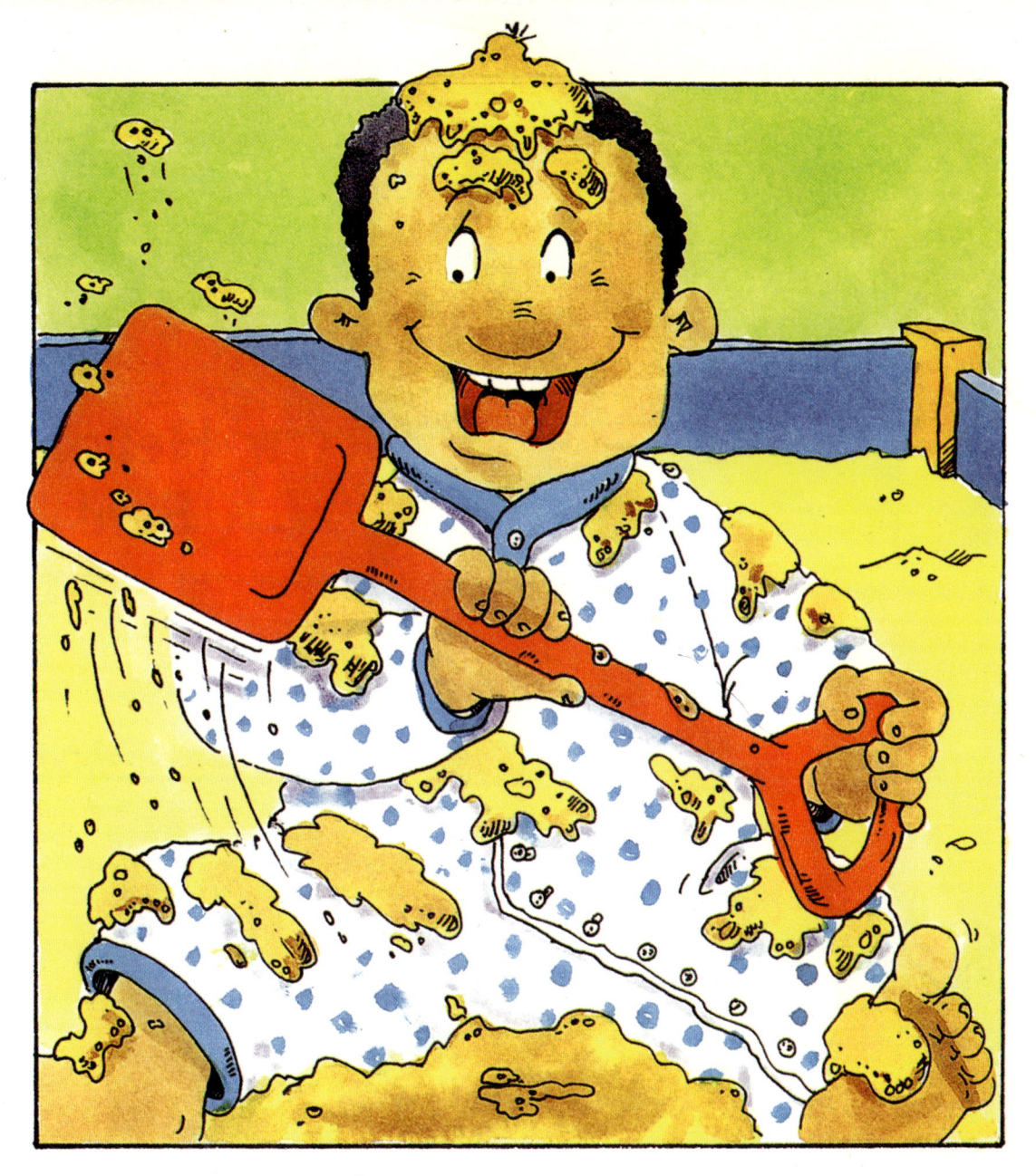

Ben had lots and lots of sand on him!

But his dad was not mad.

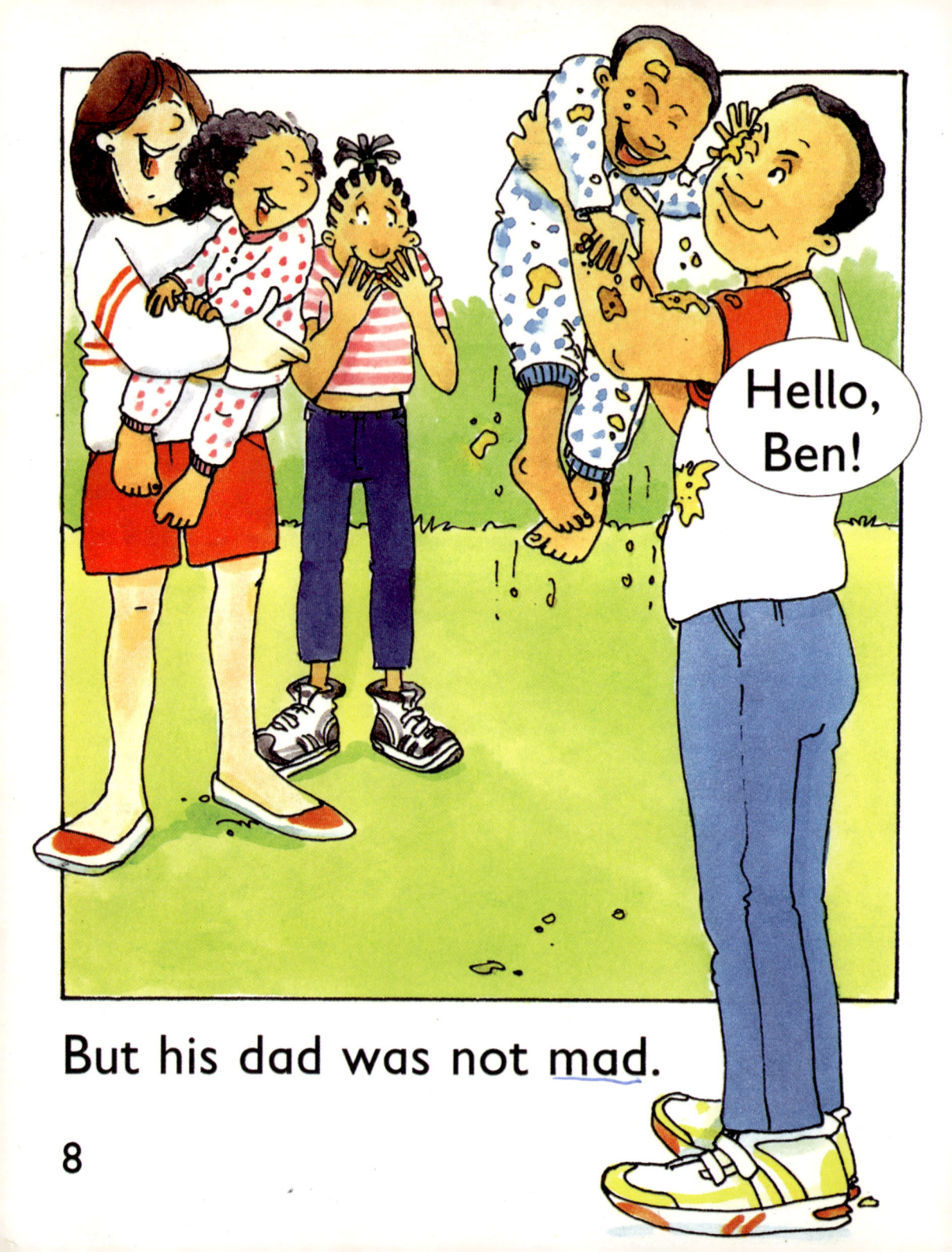

Hello, Ben!